MW01254691

Baked  Chicago's

SIMPLY DECADENT BROWNIES COOKBOOK

HARVEY MORRIS

Copyright © 2012 Baked Chicago

All rights reserved. No part of this publication may be reproduced or transmitted in any form
or by any means, electronic or mechanical, including photocopying, recording, or any other
information storage and retrieval system, without the written permission of the publisher.

Edited by Pamela Smith. Cover design and artwork by Kat Riley.

ISBN-13: 978-0615727424

For my Dad, sister Jean, and Buddy & Rhoda, my silly pugs:

Some of my favorite family memories were
created in the kitchen ... and always included you. – HJM

CONTENTS

BAKE LIKE YOU MEAN IT.™

Though I'm not a professional baker, I am absolutely a passionate one. That passion has led to some extraordinary recipes, a few deliciously simple techniques, and a lifetime of baking experiences that are as satisfying as the finished products. I'm excited to share some of them with you in my first cookbook!

Aside from my first high school job cooking in a restaurant, I bake in my home kitchen for the benefit of family (including my four pugs) and friends. And since 2007, I've enjoyed sharing recipes through my blog BakedChicago.com.

What got me started on this baking path? It may be destiny: my mother's maiden name is Baker. And like a lot of kids, I remember helping mom in the kitchen. One of my earliest baking memories is brownies from scratch, using the cooking bible of its day – the *Better Homes & Garden Cookbook* with the iconic red-and-white plaid binding. I quickly learned to experiment by throwing in my own variations like chocolate and butterscotch chips, toffee, and peanut M&Ms – all in the same dish. These early baked "masterpieces" got a warm reception at school parties. Fellow high school students dubbed my rich and unusually dense brownies "ton cake." Over the course of high school, I made a *ton* of "ton cake."

I still love tinkering with recipes and the challenge of breaking them down to the simplest terms, changing up ingredients and textures to create unique, truly flavorful treats. Here are a few truths I've discovered along the way that make my baking simple and successful:

- *Focus on fewer, high-quality ingredients in your recipes.*
- *Baking from scratch is almost always easier (and cheaper) than from a box.*
- *A recipe should be easy to follow and execute. [There's nothing I hate more than a kitchen sink full of dirty pots, pans and utensils.]*

Brownies are among the most decadent of baked deliciousness, yet deceptively easy to make and a great canvas for culinary expression. In this cookbook, you'll find 33 of my best brownie and brownie-inspired recipes. All are easy to follow with instructions fitting on a single page. I hope they inspire you to express your simply decadent baking creativity.

Baking success in the kitchen doesn't have to be hard work. Simply, ***bake like you mean it***.

~ Harvey

PEANUT BUTTER WHIRLED BROWNIES

8 T plus 4 T butter, divided

2 oz milk chocolate, chopped

4 oz semisweet chocolate, chopped

2/3 c all-purpose flour

1/2 t baking powder

3/4 c crunchy peanut butter

1/4 t plus 1/4 t salt, divided

3 eggs

2 t plus 1/2 t vanilla, divided

3/4 c granulated sugar

1/2 c confectioners' sugar

Preheat oven to 325° F. Lightly grease bottom of an 8x8-inch baking pan with butter or shortening.

In medium heatproof bowl set over pan of simmering water, stir 8 tablespoons butter plus chocolates until melted and smooth. Remove from heat and let cool slightly. In separate medium bowl, whisk together flour, baking powder and 1/4 teaspoon salt.

Take chocolate mixture and whisk in granulated sugar. Then add eggs and whisk until mixture is smooth. Stir in 2 teaspoons vanilla. Whisk in flour mixture, just until combined. Set aside.

For the peanut butter filling, stir together 4 tablespoons butter, confectioners' sugar, peanut butter, 1/4 teaspoon salt and 1/2 teaspoon vanilla in a medium bowl until smooth.

Spread 1/3 of batter in prepared baking pan. Drop dollops of peanut butter filling (1 tablespoon each) on top of batter, spaced 1 inch apart. Drizzle remaining batter on top and gently spread to fill entire pan. Drop dollops of remaining peanut butter filling on top. With a butter knife, gently swirl peanut butter filling by running knife lengthwise and crosswise through batter.

Bake for 45 minutes, or until toothpick inserted in middle comes out with a few dry crumbs. Let brownies cool completely, about 1 hour. Cut into 4 rows by 4 rows to make 16 brownies.

DECONSTRUCTED S'MORES BROWNIES

1/2 c butter	2 eggs
2 oz milk chocolate, chopped	1 t vanilla
1 c granulated sugar	3/4 c all-purpose flour
9 graham cracker squares, broken into bite-sized chunks	1 c miniature marshmallows

Preheat oven to 350° F. Lightly grease bottom of a 9x9-inch baking pan with butter or shortening.

In medium saucepan, melt the butter and chocolate over very low heat, stirring constantly. Remove from heat and stir in sugar, eggs and vanilla. Mix in flour, just until combined.

Spread half of the batter in the prepared baking pan. Sprinkle the broken graham crackers over the batter. Top the graham cracker layer with marshmallows. Spread the remaining batter on top of the marshmallows and graham crackers, cover them completely.

Bake for 25 minutes, or until set. Cool completely, about 1 hour. Cut into 4 rows by 4 rows to make 16 brownies.

Brownie Points

For a decadent twist, substitute dark chocolate for the milk chocolate.

DARK CHOCOLATE & RASPBERRY LIQUEUR BROWNIES

1/2 c butter

2 eggs

3/4 c all-purpose flour

1/2 t baking powder

1/2 t salt

1/2 c unsweetened cocoa powder

3/4 c granulated sugar

1/2 c dark brown sugar

1/2 c dark chocolate chunks

50 ml raspberry liqueur

confectioners' sugar for dusting

Preheat oven to 350° F. Lightly grease bottom of an 8x8-inch or 9x9-inch square baking pan with butter or shortening.

Melt butter in microwave-safe bowl. Add liqueur and eggs to the melted butter. Stir in all dry ingredients and mix just until blended. Spread batter in the prepared baking pan.

Bake for 30 to 35 minutes (8-inch pan) or 25-30 minutes (9-inch pan), or until the brownies are dry around edges. A toothpick inserted in the center should come out almost clean. Cool completely, about 1 hour.

Lightly dust brownies with confectioners' sugar and cut into 4 rows by 4 rows to make 16 brownies.

Brownie Points

Change the flavor profile by substituting the raspberry liqueur with your favorite flavored liqueur, such as coffee, Irish cream, black currant or orange.

SPICY CINNAMON HAZELNUT BROWNIES

1/4 c butter

3 eggs

1 1/4 c all-purpose flour

1 t baking powder

1/8 t salt

1/2 c unsweetened cocoa powder

1 c granulated sugar

1/2 c dark chocolate chunks

1/4 t ground cinnamon

1/8 t cayenne pepper

1/3 c cold water

3 T vegetable oil

1 t vanilla

1/2 c hazelnuts, chopped

cinnamon-sugar mixture for dusting

Preheat oven to 350° F. Lightly grease bottom of a 9x9-inch square baking pan with butter or shortening.

Melt butter in a medium-sized saucepan and then remove from heat. Stir in sugar and water first, then eggs, oil and vanilla. Stir in all dry ingredients (except dark chocolate chunks) and mix just until blended. Fold in dark chocolate chunks and hazelnuts. Spread batter in the prepared baking pan.

Bake for 25 minutes, or until a toothpick inserted in the center comes out clean. Cool completely, about 1 hour.

Dust brownies with a cinnamon-sugar mix and cut into 4 rows by 4 rows to make 16 brownies.

Brownie Points

Substitute espresso powder for the cayenne pepper for a less spicy option.

COOKIE CRUNCH BROWNIES

4 oz dark chocolate, chopped

3/4 c butter

1 c granulated sugar

3 eggs

1 t vanilla

1/4 t salt

1 c all-purpose flour

12 sandwich cookies, chopped

Preheat oven to 350° F. Lightly grease bottom of an 8x8-inch baking pan with butter or shortening.

In medium saucepan, stir dark chocolate and butter over medium-low heat until melted and smooth. Remove from heat and stir in sugar, eggs, vanilla and salt. Gradually add flour and stir, just until combined. Fold in cookies.

Spread batter in the prepared baking pan. Bake for 30 minutes. Cool completely, about 1 hour. Cut into 3 rows by 3 rows to make 9 brownies.

PEANUT BUTTER & JELLY (PB&J) BROWNIES

1/4 c butter, softened

2 eggs

1/2 c all-purpose flour

6 oz dark chocolate, chopped

1 c dark brown sugar

1/2 c crunchy peanut butter

1/2 c jam

1 t vanilla

1/4 t salt

Preheat oven to 350° F. Lightly grease bottom of a 9x9-inch square baking pan with butter or shortening.

Beat butter, brown sugar and peanut butter in large bowl with electric mixer on medium speed until well blended. Add eggs and vanilla, and then mix well. Beat in flour and salt until well blended. Fold in chopped dark chocolate.

Spread batter in the prepared baking pan. Drop jam by spoonfuls over batter, and then swirl into the batter with a butter knife to create a marble effect. Bake for 35 to 40 minutes, or until a toothpick inserted in the center comes out almost clean. Cool completely, about 1 hour.

Lightly dust with cinnamon-sugar mixture and cut into 6 rows by 4 rows to make 24 brownies.

Brownie Points

Jam is better for baking than jelly because it includes pieces of actual fruit, whereas, jelly is made up of only fruit juices. Use any of your favorite jams for this recipe. For a stronger flavor contrast against the dark chocolate, try strawberry, raspberry or apricot jam.

BANANA CREAM BROWNIES

8 oz dark chocolate, chopped

3/4 c butter, cut into small pieces

1 1/4 c granulated sugar

4 eggs

3/4 c plus 1 T all-purpose flour,
   divided

pinch of salt

1 egg yolk

1/4 c confectioners' sugar

1/2 t vanilla

1 very ripe banana, mashed

8 oz cream cheese, room
   temperature

Preheat oven to 350° F. Lightly grease bottom of a 9x13-inch baking pan with butter or shortening. In medium saucepan, bring water to a boil. Remove from heat. Put dark chocolate in heatproof bowl and set it over saucepan. Stir until chocolate is completely melted.

Use electric mixer with paddle attachment to beat butter and sugar in a bowl on medium-low speed. Mix until light and fluffy (3 minutes). Add 3 eggs. Beat to combine. Add in chocolate mixture, 3/4 cup flour and salt. Mix until just combined.

In food processor, blend cream cheese until smooth and creamy (30 seconds). Add egg yolk, confectioners' sugar, vanilla, remaining tablespoon of flour and egg. Process until smooth (1 minute). Transfer to a bowl and fold in the mashed banana.

Spread chocolate batter into prepared baking pan. Using a rubber spatula, make three trenches in the batter and fill with banana cream cheese mixture. To create marble effect, run tip of a knife back and forth through the batters.

Bake for 40 minutes, or until set. Cool completely. Cut into 4 rows by 8 rows to make 32 brownies.

CHERRY CABERNET BROWNIES

3/4 c cold butter

3 eggs

1 c all-purpose flour

4 oz dark chocolate, chopped

2 c granulated sugar

1/2 c Cabernet Sauvignon wine

1 c dried cherries, chopped

1 t vanilla

1/4 t salt

1/2 t baking powder

1/4 t baking soda

Preheat oven to 350° F. Lightly grease bottom of a 13x9-inch baking pan with butter or shortening. Set aside.

In small saucepan, combine dried cherries and 1/2 cup Cabernet Sauvignon. Bring to a boil and remove from heat. Set aside.

In medium saucepan, stir 3/4 cup butter and baking chocolate over low heat until melted and smooth. Whisk in sugar. Then add eggs one at a time, whisking well after each addition. Stir in vanilla.

In small bowl, stir together flour, baking powder, baking soda and salt. Stir dry mixture into chocolate mixture until combined. Fold in cherries and wine mixture.

Spread batter in the prepared baking pan. Bake for 35 minutes, or until sides pull away from the pan. Cool completely, about 1 hour. Cut into 24 bars.

Brownie Points

Chocolate scorches easily, so don't be tempted to increase the heat in order to speed the melting process.

NO-BOWL-NEEDED GINGER BROWNIES

1/2 c butter	1 t fresh ginger, grated, peeled
3 oz dark chocolate, chopped	1/2 t vanilla
1 c granulated sugar	1/2 t ground nutmeg
2/3 c all-purpose flour	1/2 t ground ginger
1/4 c unsweetened cocoa powder	1/4 t salt
2 eggs	1/8 t ground cloves

Preheat oven to 325° F. Lightly grease bottom of an 8x8-inch baking pan with butter or shortening.

In medium saucepan, stir dark chocolate and butter over medium-low heat until melted and smooth. Remove from heat and stir in remaining ingredients.

Spread batter in the prepared baking pan. Bake for 30 to 35 minutes, or until a toothpick inserted in the center comes out with moist crumbs. Cool completely, about 1 hour. Cut into 4 rows by 4 rows to make 16 brownies.

Brownie Points

For a crunchier texture, either mix 10 ginger snap cookies (broken into small pieces) into the batter or sprinkle on top before baking.

ROOT BEER BROWNIES

2/3 c all-purpose flour	4 T butter
1/2 c unsweetened cocoa powder	3 eggs
1/2 t salt	1 c granulated sugar
8 oz dark chocolate, chopped	1 t vanilla
8 oz root beer	

Preheat oven to 350° F. Lightly grease bottom of a 9x9-inch baking pan with butter or shortening.

In small bowl, mix together flour, cocoa powder and salt. Set aside.

In small saucepan, melt the butter and dark chocolate over very low heat, stirring constantly until mixture is smooth. Set aside to cool slightly.

In large bowl, beat together eggs and sugar until well combined. Blend in cooled chocolate mixture. Stir in half of flour mixture, followed by half of root beer. Stir in remaining flour mixture, remaining root beer and vanilla, just until combined.

Spread the batter in the prepared baking pan. Bake for 25 to 30 minutes, or until a toothpick inserted in the center comes out nearly clean. Cool completely, about 1 hour. Cut into 4 rows by 4 rows to make 16 brownies.

Brownie Points

These brownies are fudgier, moister and have a deeper root beer flavor the day after baking. Wrap tight and store in the refrigerator overnight.

BROWNIE COOKIES

12 oz dark chocolate, chopped	1/2 c granulated sugar
1/2 c all-purpose flour	1/2 c dark brown sugar
1/4 t baking powder	3 eggs
1/4 t salt	1 t vanilla
6 T butter	1 c milk chocolate chunks

Preheat oven to 350° F. Place dark chocolate in a heatproof bowl over a saucepan of simmering water. Stir until melted; set aside and let cool.

In small bowl, stir together flour, baking powder and salt. Set aside. In a separate large bowl, use a mixer to beat together butter and sugars (about 2 minutes). Add eggs and vanilla, beating until combined. With mixer on low speed, alternately beat in chocolate and flour mixtures. Mix just until combined. Fold in milk chocolate chunks.

Drop dough by heaping tablespoons, about 2 inches apart, onto parchment-lined baking sheets. Bake for 14 to 16 minutes. Transfer to wire rack and cool completely. Yields about 32 cookies.

Brownie Points

Brownie cookies are great for making homemade ice cream sandwiches. Scoop softened vanilla ice cream between two warm cookies for a memorable treat!

MARBLED PUMPKIN PECAN BROWNIES

1/2 c butter

6 oz dark chocolate, chopped

2 c all-purpose flour

1 t baking powder

1/2 t salt

1 3/4 c granulated sugar

4 eggs

1 T vanilla

1 1/4 c canned pumpkin

1/4 c vegetable oil

1 t ground cinnamon

1/4 t ground nutmeg

1/2 c pecans, chopped

Preheat oven to 350° F. Lightly grease bottom of a 9x9-inch baking pan with butter or shortening. Melt dark chocolate and butter in heatproof bowl, set over a pan of simmering water. Stir constantly until melted and smooth.

In large bowl, whisk together flour, baking powder and salt. Set aside. In stand mixer with paddle attachment, mix sugar, eggs and vanilla. Beat until fluffy. Beat in the flour mixture.

Divide batter in half between two bowls. Stir chocolate mixture into one bowl. In the other bowl, stir in pumpkin, oil, cinnamon, nutmeg and pecans. Transfer half chocolate batter to the prepared baking pan. Then top with half the pumpkin batter. Repeat one more chocolate layer and one pumpkin layer. Using butter knife, gently swirl the two batters to create marbled effect.

Bake for 40 to 45 minutes, or until set. Let brownies cool completely, about 1 hour. Cut into 4 rows by 4 rows to make 16 brownies.

Brownie Points

Canned pumpkin contains only pureed pumpkin or squash with low salt. Use this rather than pumpkin pie filling which has added sugar and spices.

DARK CHOCOLATE FLOURLESS BROWNIES

1/4 c unsweetened cocoa powder	1 1/4 c dark chocolate, chopped
1/4 t baking soda	4 eggs
1/4 t salt	1/2 c cold water
1 c butter, cut into small pieces	1 t vanilla
1 1/4 c granulated sugar	1/3 c semi-sweet chocolate chips

Preheat oven to 350° F. Lightly grease bottom of an 8x8-inch square baking pan with butter or shortening.

In medium bowl, whisk together cocoa powder, baking soda and salt. Set aside.

In large heatproof bowl, combine butter, sugar and dark chocolate. Place bowl over simmering water in saucepan. Stirring often, heat until butter and chocolate are melted and mixture is smooth. Remove from heat and whisk in eggs, water and vanilla. Stir in cocoa powder mixture; fold in chocolate chips.

Spread batter in the prepared baking pan. Bake for 40 to 55 minutes, or until a toothpick inserted in the center comes out clean. Cool completely, about 1 hour.

Lightly dust with powdered sugar and cut into 4 rows by 4 rows to make 16 brownies.

GINGERBREAD BROWNIES

1/4 c butter	1/2 c dark chocolate chunks
2 eggs	1 t ground cinnamon
1 1/2 c all-purpose flour	1 t ground ginger
1/2 t baking soda	1/2 t ground cloves
1/4 c unsweetened cocoa powder	1/3 c molasses
1 c granulated sugar	confectioners' sugar for dusting

Preheat oven to 350° F. Lightly grease bottom of a 13x9-inch baking pan with butter or shortening.

In large mixing bowl, combine flour, sugar, cocoa powder, ginger, cinnamon, cloves and baking soda. Set aside. Melt butter in microwave-safe bowl. Add molasses and eggs to the melted butter. Add wet ingredients to flour mixture and stir just until blended. Fold in dark chocolate chunks.

Spread batter in the prepared baking pan. Bake for 20 minutes. The center should be slightly firm to the touch. Cool completely, about 1 hour.

Dust with confectioners' sugar and cut into 6 rows by 4 rows to make 24 brownies.

Brownie Points

It's easy to turn this recipe into a holiday breakfast muffin. Spoon batter into paper-lined muffin cups until about 2/3 full. Then bake at 325° F for 20 minutes.

CAPPUCCINO BROWNIES

1/2 c butter

4 oz unsweetened chocolate, chopped

1 1/2 c granulated sugar

1 c all-purpose flour

2 t vanilla

3/4 c dark chocolate chips

4 eggs

1 T instant espresso powder

3/4 t ground cinnamon

1/2 t ground nutmeg

1/4 t salt

Preheat oven to 325° F. Lightly grease bottom of a 9x9-inch square baking pan with butter or shortening.

In large saucepan, melt unsweetened chocolate and butter over very low heat. Stir constantly until completely melted. Remove from heat and whisk in sugar, espresso powder and vanilla. Add eggs after mixture has slightly cooled.

In medium bowl, whisk together flour, cinnamon, nutmeg and salt. Add flour mixture to the chocolate mixture. Stir until just combined and then fold in dark chocolate chips.

Spread batter in the prepared baking pan. Bake for 30 to 35 minutes, or until a toothpick inserted in the center comes out almost clean. Cool completely, about 1 hour. Cut into 4 rows by 4 rows to make 16 brownies.

Brownie Points

If you don't have instant espresso powder, substitute instant coffee powder – preferably a dark roast.

CHIPOTLE-CHOCOLATE BROWNIES

8 oz dark chocolate, chopped

1 c butter

2 c all-purpose flour

1/4 c unsweetened cocoa powder

2 1/2 c granulated sugar

1 1/2 t ground cinnamon

1 t ground chipotle powder

6 eggs

2 t vanilla

1 T instant espresso coffee powder

Preheat oven to 325° F. Lightly grease bottom of a 13x9-inch baking pan with butter or shortening.

In small saucepan, combine dark chocolate and butter. Stir constantly over very low heat until melted and smooth. Cool slightly. In small bowl, combine flour and cocoa powder; set aside.

In large bowl, combine sugar, espresso coffee powder, cinnamon and chipotle powder. Add in the chocolate mixture. Beat with mixer on medium speed for 1 minute. Add eggs, one at a time, beating on low speed after each addition just until combined. Mix in vanilla. Add flour mixture, a half cup at a time, beating on low speed just until combined.

Spread batter in the prepared baking pan. Bake for 35 to 40 minutes, or until edges start to pull away from sides of pan. Cool completely, about 1 hour.

Dust with unsweetened cocoa powder and cut into 8 rows by 4 rows to make 32 brownies.

Brownie Points

If you want more heat, increase ground chipotle powder to 2 teaspoons.

APPLE CARAMEL BROWNIES

1/2 c butter

1 egg

1 c all-purpose flour

1 t ground cinnamon

1/2 t baking powder

2 3/4 c Granny Smith apples, cored, peeled and cut into 1/2-inch cubes (about 2 large apples)

30 soft caramel candies, unwrapped

1/4 t baking soda

1/2 t salt

1 c granulated sugar

1 t vanilla

1/2 c peanuts (salted and skinless), chopped

Preheat oven to 350° F. Lightly grease bottom of a 9x9-inch baking pan with butter or shortening. Set aside.

In medium bowl, stir together flour, cinnamon, baking powder, salt and baking soda. Set aside. In a separate bowl, use a mixer to beat together butter, sugar and egg (about 2 minutes). Fold in apples and caramels by hand until combined. Add the flour mixture and stir until combined.

Spread batter in the prepared baking pan. Sprinkle chopped peanuts on top. Bake for 40 minutes, or until golden brown and slightly firm. Cool completely, about 1 hour. Cut into 16 bars.

Brownie Points

Granny Smith apples, available year round, provide a tart contrast to the sweetness of the caramel. Try this recipe with Honeycrisp apples, available in the fall, for a richer, smoother flavor.

TOFFEE SHORTBREAD BROWNIES

1/4 c dark brown sugar

1/2 c and 1/3 c butter, divided

1/4 c toffee bits

1 1/3 c granulated sugar

1/2 c dark chocolate chunks

1 c and 3/4 c all-purpose flour,
   divided

1/2 c unsweetened cocoa powder

1 1/2 t baking powder

1/2 t salt

3 eggs

1 T vanilla

Preheat oven to 350° F. Lightly grease bottom of a 9x9-inch baking pan with butter or shortening.

In medium bowl, stir together 1 cup flour and dark brown sugar. Cut in 1/2 cup butter until mixture resembles coarse crumbs. Stir in toffee bits. Press into the prepared baking pan. Bake for 8 minutes.

Meanwhile, in large bowl, stir together sugar, 3/4 cup flour, cocoa powder, baking powder and salt. Add eggs, vanilla and remaining 1/3 cup butter (melted). Beat until smooth. Stir in dark chocolate chunks.

After removing baking pan from oven, carefully spread the brownie filling batter over the shortbread crust.

Bake for 40 minutes more. Let brownies cool completely, about 1 hour. Cut into 4 rows by 4 rows to make 16 brownies.

BACON & SALTED CARAMEL BROWNIES

4 slices of bacon

1/2 c heavy cream

1/4 c unsweetened cocoa powder

1 c plus 1 c granulated sugar, divided

6 T plus 1/2 c salted butter, divided
  and cut into pieces

3 eggs

1 t vanilla

1 c all-purpose flour

6 oz dark chocolate, finely chopped

In medium skillet, fry bacon slices until crisp. Remove bacon, reserving the bacon grease in the pan. Add cream to pan and let cool. When bacon has cooled, crumble or chop finely.

In medium saucepan, heat 1 cup sugar over high heat until the mixture is liquid and deep amber in color. Add 6 tablespoons butter and cooled bacon cream mixture. Stir until butter is melted. Add chopped bacon and let cool.

Preheat oven to 350° F. Lightly grease bottom of an 8x8-inch baking pan with butter or shortening.

In large saucepan, melt remaining butter and dark chocolate over very low heat, stirring constantly. Remove from heat and stir in cocoa powder. Whisk until smooth and add in eggs, one at a time. Mix in remaining sugar, vanilla and flour, just until combined.

Spread half the brownie batter in the prepared baking pan. Drop half the bacon caramel mixture by tablespoon, evenly spaced, over the brownie batter. Spread remaining brownie batter over the top, and then drop remaining bacon caramel mixture by spoonfuls over the top of the brownies. Drag the back of the tablespoon through the batter to create a swirled effect.

Bake for 35 to 40 minutes. Cool completely, about 1 hour. Cut into 4 rows by 4 rows to make 16 brownies.

PEPPERMINT BROWNIES

8 oz dark chocolate, chopped	3 1/2 c granulated sugar
1 c butter, cut into cubes	1 2/3 c all-purpose flour
5 eggs, at room temperature	6 peppermint candy canes, crushed
2 t vanilla	1/4 t salt
1 T instant espresso powder	1 lb chocolate-covered peppermint- flavored patties, unwrapped

Preheat oven to 425° F. Lightly grease bottom of a 9x13-inch baking pan with butter or shortening.

In medium heatproof bowl, set over pan of simmering water, stir dark chocolate and butter until melted and smooth. Remove from heat and set aside.

In bowl of stand mixer fitted with whisk attachment, whip eggs, vanilla, salt, espresso powder and sugar on high speed until foamy and stiff (about 10 minutes).

Stir in the chocolate mixture by hand, followed by the flour.

Spread half the batter in the prepared baking pan. Place a layer of peppermint patties candies over the batter. Pour remaining batter over the peppermint patties and smooth the top. Sprinkle crushed candy canes over top of brownies.

Bake for 20 to 22 minutes, or until a firm crust is formed on top. A toothpick inserted in the center should come out moist. Cool completely, about 1 hour. Cut into 8 rows by 4 rows to make 32 brownies.

BOURBON, BACON & PECAN BROWNIES

6 slices of bacon

2 c all-purpose flour

1 t salt

10 oz dark chocolate, chopped

1/2 c pecans, chopped

2 T unsweetened cocoa powder

1/2 c butter

4 eggs

1 c granulated sugar

1/2 c dark brown sugar

3 T bourbon

In medium skillet, cook the bacon until crispy. Reserve 1/4 cup of the bacon fat and set aside. Let bacon cool and chop roughly. Set aside.

Preheat oven to 350° F. Lightly grease bottom of a 9x9-inch baking pan with butter or shortening.

In medium bowl, mix together flour, cocoa powder and salt. Set aside.

In large heatproof bowl set on top of small saucepan of simmering water, melt dark chocolate and butter. Stir constantly, until smooth. Remove from heat and cool slightly.

With electric mixer on medium-low speed, beat eggs, granulated sugar, and brown sugar until frothy (about 1 minute). Beat in melted chocolate mixture, bourbon and reserved bacon fat. Fold in flour mixture and pecans, just until combined.

Spread the batter in the prepared baking pan. Sprinkle bacon on top. Bake for 35 to 40 minutes, or until a toothpick inserted in the center comes out nearly clean. Cool completely, about 1 hour. Cut into 4 rows by 4 rows to make 16 brownies.

STOUT-GLAZED BROWNIES

1 c stout	3 eggs
3/4 c all-purpose flour	1 t vanilla
1 c plus 2 T butter, divided	12 oz plus 4 oz dark chocolate, chopped, divided
1 1/2 c granulated sugar	1 1/4 t and 1/4 t salt, divided

Preheat oven to 350° F. Lightly grease bottom of a 9x9-inch baking pan with butter or shortening. In medium saucepan, bring stout to a boil and cook until reduced to 1/2 cup (about 10 minutes). Let cool and set aside.

In medium heatproof bowl set on small saucepan of simmering water, melt 12 ounces dark chocolate and 1 cup butter. Stir constantly, until smooth. Remove from heat and cool slightly.

Whisk sugar, eggs and vanilla in a large bowl. Gradually whisk in chocolate mixture and 1/4 cup stout, reserving remaining stout. Fold in flour and 1 1/4 teaspoons salt.

Spread batter in prepared baking pan. Bake for 35 to 40 minutes, or until surface begins to crack. Toothpick inserted in center should come out with moist crumbs. Cool for 20 minutes.

Stir remaining 4 ounces of dark chocolate in medium heatproof bowl, set on top of small saucepan of simmering water, until melted and smooth. Add reserved 1/4 cup stout, remaining 2 tablespoons butter and remaining 1/4 teaspoon salt. Whisk until well blended.

Pour warm glaze over brownies. Let stand until glaze is set (about 40 minutes). Cut into 4 rows by 4 rows to make 16 brownies.

GERMAN CHOCOLATE BROWNIES

4 oz dark chocolate, chopped	1/4 t salt
1/2 c evaporated milk	1 c all-purpose flour
1 c and 1/2 c granulated sugar, divided	1 t plus 1 t vanilla, divided
3 eggs and 1 egg yolk, divided	1/2 c toasted pecans, chopped
3/4 c plus 4 T butter, divided	1/2 c toasted coconut flakes

Preheat oven to 350° F. Lightly grease bottom of an 8x8-inch baking pan with butter or shortening.

In medium saucepan, stir dark chocolate and 3/4 cup butter over medium-low heat until melted and smooth. Remove from heat. Whisk in 1 cup of sugar, 3 eggs, 1 teaspoon vanilla and salt. Gradually add in flour, stirring just until combined. Spread batter in the prepared baking pan. Bake for 30 to 35 minutes. Let brownies cool completely, about 1 hour.

Prepare frosting by combining evaporated milk, 1/2 cup sugar, egg yolk and 4 tablespoons butter in large saucepan. Cook over low heat, stirring constantly until thickened (about 5 minutes). Remove from heat and stir in 1 teaspoon vanilla, pecans and coconut. While frosting is still warm, spread on brownies. Cut into 4 rows by 4 rows to make 16 brownies.

Brownie Points

Evaporated milk is milk that's been cooked down to allow water content to evaporate. The concentrate is canned, and the result is heavier, creamier milk with a slightly toasted or caramelized flavor. If you don't have evaporated milk in the pantry, make your own! To produce 1 cup of evaporated milk, simmer 2 1/4 cups of regular milk in a small saucepan over medium-low heat until it reduces to 1 cup.

WHITE CHOCOLATE PECAN BROWNIES

6 T butter

2 eggs

1/4 c granulated sugar

6 oz plus 2 oz white baking
    chocolate, chopped, divided

1 c all-purpose flour

1/2 t vanilla

1/2 c pecans, chopped

Preheat oven to 350° F. Lightly grease bottom of an 8x8-inch baking pan with butter or shortening.

In small, heavy saucepan, combine 6 ounces white chocolate and butter. Cook over low heat, stirring until melted. Remove from heat and let cool for 10 minutes.

In medium bowl, add eggs and sugar. Stir in white chocolate mixture with a spatula, just until combined. Add in flour and vanilla, stirring just until smooth. Fold in pecans.

Spread batter in the prepared baking pan. Bake for 25 minutes, or until top is lightly golden. Immediately sprinkle remaining 2 ounces of white chocolate over brownies. As white chocolate melts, use spatula to spread it over brownies.

Let brownies cool completely, about 1 hour. Cut into 4 rows by 4 rows to make 16 brownies.

PEANUT BUTTER BROWNIE BISCOTTI

1/3 c crunchy peanut butter

1/4 c butter, softened

2/3 c granulated sugar

1/3 c unsweetened cocoa powder

1 1/2 t baking powder

2 eggs

1 t vanilla

1 3/4 c all-purpose flour

1 c dark chocolate, chopped

Preheat oven to 375° F. In large bowl, combine peanut butter and butter. Beat with electric mixer on medium speed for 1 minute. Add sugar, cocoa powder and baking powder. Beat until combined. Add eggs and vanilla, beating just until combined.

Use the mixer to incorporate about half of the flour before using a wooden spoon to stir in the remaining flour by hand. Fold in the dark chocolate.

Transfer dough to a lightly floured surface and divide the dough in half. Shape each dough portion into a 9-inch long log roll. Place rolls 3 inches apart on a large, ungreased cookie sheet. Flatten the rolls slightly, to about 2 inches wide.

Bake initially for 20 to 25 minutes, or until a toothpick inserted in the center comes out clean. Let cool on the cookie sheet for 1 hour.

Preheat oven to 325° F. Transfer the baked loaves to a cutting board. Using a serrated knife, cut each loaf diagonally into 1/2-inch thick slices. Place slices on ungreased cookie sheets. Bake for 10 minutes, before turning slices over. Bake for 10 to 12 minutes more, or until biscotti are dry and crisp. Transfer biscotti to wire racks to cool completely. Makes about 32 biscotti.

MALTED BROWNIES

1 c butter, cut into small chunks

1 c all-purpose flour

1 c malted milk powder

10 oz semisweet chocolate, chopped

1 c malted milk balls, crushed

1 1/2 c dark brown sugar

3 eggs

1 T vanilla

Preheat oven to 350° F. Lightly grease bottom of a 9x13-inch baking pan with butter or shortening.

In medium saucepan, stir semisweet chocolate and butter over medium-low heat until melted and smooth. Remove from heat and set aside.

In medium bowl, whisk together flour, malted milk powder and malted milk balls. Set aside.

In the bowl of a stand mixer fitted with a whisk attachment, beat sugar and eggs together until thick and fluffy (about 2 minutes). Add melted chocolate mixture and vanilla. Mix to combine. Using a spatula, fold in the flour mixture, just until combined.

Spread batter in the prepared baking pan. Bake for 30 to 35 minutes, or until toothpick inserted in center comes out with a few moist crumbs. Cool completely, about 1 hour. Cut into 8 rows by 4 rows to make 32 brownies.

Brownie Points

For a mess-free way to crush malted milk balls, place them in a re-sealable plastic freezer bag. Whack the freezer bag a few times with a rolling pin. Then push the rolling pin over the top of the bag, back and forth, until you have the desired consistency.

BUTTERMILK BROWNIES

2 c all-purpose flour	1 c butter
2 c granulated sugar	1/3 c unsweetened cocoa powder
1 t baking soda	2 eggs
1/4 t salt	1/2 c buttermilk
1 c water	1 1/2 t vanilla

Preheat oven to 350° F. Lightly grease bottom of a 13x9-inch baking pan with butter or shortening.

In medium bowl, combine flour, sugar, baking soda and salt. Set aside.

In medium saucepan, combine water, butter and cocoa powder. Bring mixture to a boil, stirring constantly. Remove from heat. Add the cocoa mixture to the flour mixture. Beat with an electric mixer on medium speed until combined. Add in eggs, buttermilk and vanilla. Beat for 1 minute.

Spread batter in the prepared baking pan. Bake for 35 minutes, or until toothpick inserted in center comes out clean. Let brownies cool completely, about 1 hour. Cut into 6 rows by 4 rows to make 24 brownies.

MARSHMALLOW PRETZEL CRUNCH BROWNIES

10 T butter

1 3/4 c dark brown sugar

3/4 c unsweetened cocoa powder, sifted

1 c all-purpose flour

1 t baking soda

2 c and 1/2 c pretzel twists or sticks, coarsely chopped, divided

1 t vanilla

4 eggs

pinch of salt

1/2 c salted peanuts, chopped

1 c miniature marshmallows

1 c and 1/2 c milk chocolate chips, divided

Preheat oven to 375° F. Lightly grease bottom of a 13x9-inch baking pan with butter or shortening.

Whisk together in large bowl the cocoa powder, flour, baking powder and salt. Then set aside.

Melt butter in a medium saucepan over low heat. Add dark brown sugar, stirring until completely blended with butter. Stir flour mixture into the butter mixture. When mixed, remove from heat and set aside. The mixture at this point will be very dry.

In medium bowl, whisk eggs and vanilla. Incorporate egg mixture into brownie batter in the pan. Fold in 2 cups pretzels and 1 cup milk chocolate chips. Pour into the prepared baking pan.

In medium bowl, stir together marshmallows, peanuts, 1/2 cup pretzels and 1/2 cup milk chocolate chips. Sprinkle evenly over the top of brownie batter.

Bake for 25 minutes, or until set. Let brownies cool completely, about 1 hour. Cut into 6 rows by 4 rows to make 24 brownies.

BUTTERSCOTCH BROWNIES

1/3 c and 1/2 c butter, divided	1/4 t salt
1/2 t baking soda	3 eggs
1/2 c miniature marshmallows	1/2 t vanilla
1 1/3 c shredded coconut	1 1/2 c all-purpose flour
3/4 c and 1/2 c pecans, chopped, divided	2/3 c and 1 c dark brown sugar, divided

Preheat oven to 350° F. Lightly grease bottom of a 13x9-inch baking pan with butter or shortening. In small saucepan, melt 1/3 cup butter. Stir in 2/3 cup dark brown sugar, coconut and 3/4 cup pecans. Pat evenly into the prepared baking pan and set aside.

In large bowl, beat 1/2 cup butter with electric mixer on medium-high speed. Add 1 cup dark brown sugar, baking soda and salt. Beat until combined. Beat in eggs and vanilla, just until combined. Add flour and beat until combined. Fold in 1/2 cup pecans and marshmallows.

Carefully spread over coconut mixture in baking pan. Bake for 20 minutes, or until top is evenly golden brown. Let brownies cool completely, about 1 hour. Cut into 6 rows by 4 rows to make 24 brownies.

Brownie Points

Create a Butterscotch Brownie Banana Split: Put two warm brownies on the bottom of a bowl, then layer with slices of banana and your favorite ice cream. Top it off with caramel sauce. Yum!

WARM BROWNIE PUDDING CUPS

1/2 c butter	1/2 c unsweetened cocoa powder
1/2 c all-purpose flour	4 eggs, room temperature
1/2 t baking powder	1 t vanilla
pinch of salt	1 c granulated sugar
4 oz semisweet chocolate, chopped	confectioners' sugar for dusting

Preheat oven to 350° F. Place a baking pan half full of water in the oven to get warm.

In medium heatproof bowl over saucepan of simmering water, stir semisweet chocolate and butter until almost melted and smooth. Remove from heat and let cool, stirring occasionally.

In medium bowl, sift together twice the flour, baking powder, salt, and cocoa powder. Set aside.

In separate medium bowl, beat eggs and vanilla until light and foamy. Add in sugar and beat until fluffy. Stir in the chocolate mixture, and then fold in dry ingredients.

Pour batter into five 8-ounce ramekins, filling each nearly to the rim. Place ramekins in the baking pan. Water should come halfway up the sides of ramekins.

Bake for 30 minutes, or until brownies have risen to just above the rim and tops are cracked. They should be firm to the touch. Let cool for 5 minutes, and then dust with confectioners' sugar. Serve warm.

TURTLE BROWNIES

1/4 c butter	2 eggs
3 oz dark chocolate, chopped	1/4 c whole milk
1/2 t plus 1/2 t salt, divided	1 t plus 1 t vanilla, divided
1/4 t baking powder	1/3 c heavy cream
1/2 c all-purpose flour	1 c toasted pecans, chopped
1 c plus 1 c granulated sugar, divided	1/3 c water

Preheat oven to 325° F. Lightly grease bottom of an 8x8-inch baking pan with butter or shortening. Melt dark chocolate and butter in heatproof bowl, set over pan of simmering water. Stir constantly until melted and smooth. Let cool slightly.

Whisk together in a large bowl flour, baking powder and salt. Set aside. Whisk sugar and eggs on medium speed with electric mixer until pale and fluffy (4 minutes). Add chocolate mixture, milk and vanilla, mixing until combined. Reduce speed to low and add flour mixture, until well combined.

Pour batter into prepared baking pan. Bake for 28 to 30 minutes, or until toothpick inserted comes out with a few dry crumbs. Let brownies cool, about 30 minutes.

Bring 1/3 cup water and 1 cup sugar to a boil in medium saucepan over medium-high heat. Constantly stir until sugar has dissolved. Wash down sides of the pan with a wet pastry brush to prevent sugar crystals from forming. Cook until sugar is medium amber color (5 to 7 minutes). Remove from heat and add heavy cream, 1 teaspoon vanilla and 1/2 teaspoon salt. Gently stir with wooden spoon until smooth. Add pecans and stir until caramel begins to cool and thicken.

Spread caramel over brownies. Refrigerate for one hour to help set. Let brownies stand at room temperature for 15 minutes before serving. Cut into 4 rows by 4 rows to make 16 brownies.

RED VELVET BROWNIES

4 oz semisweet chocolate, chopped

3/4 c plus 3 T butter, divided

2 c granulated sugar

4 eggs

1 1/2 c all-purpose flour

1 1/2 t baking powder

1 t plus 1 t vanilla, divided

1/8 t plus 1/8 t salt, divided

8 oz cream cheese, softened

1 1/2 c confectioners' sugar

1 oz red food coloring

Preheat oven to 350° F. Lightly grease bottom of a 9x9-inch baking pan with butter or shortening.

In medium heatproof bowl over saucepan of simmering water, stir semisweet chocolate and 3/4 cup butter until melted and smooth. Whisk in granulated sugar. Add eggs, one at a time, whisking just until combined. Gently stir in flour, red food coloring, baking powder, 1 teaspoon vanilla and 1/8 teaspoon salt.

Spread batter in prepared baking pan. Bake for 40 to 45 minutes, or until toothpick inserted comes out with moist crumbs. Let brownies cool completely, about 1 hour.

While brownies are cooling, prepare cream cheese frosting. In medium bowl, use electric mixer on medium speed to beat cream cheese and remaining butter until creamy. Gradually add in confectioners' sugar and 1/8 teaspoon salt, beating until blended. Stir in vanilla.

Spread frosting on top of brownies. Cut into 4 rows by 4 rows to make 16 brownies.

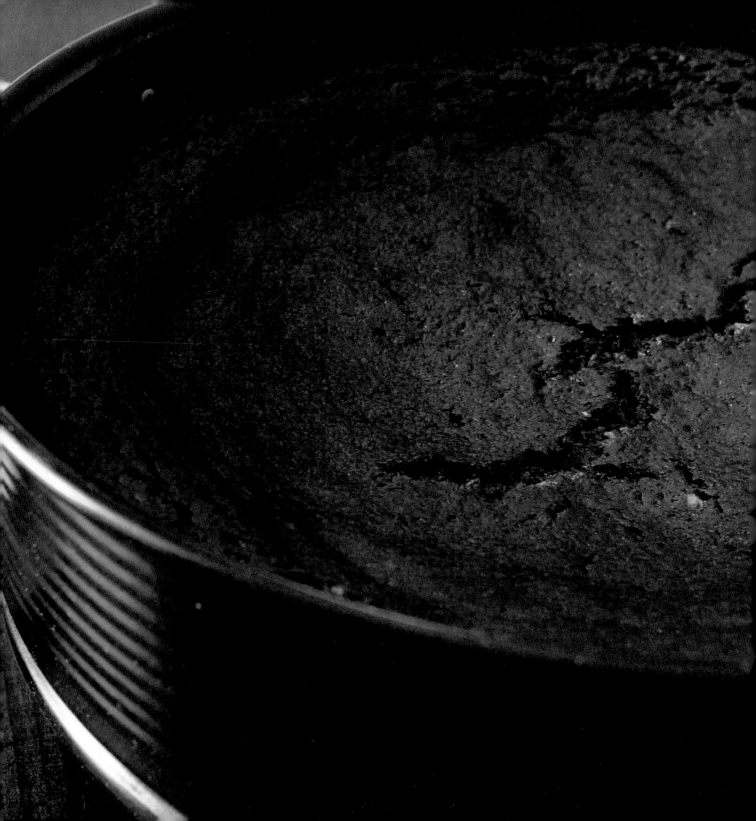

BROWNIE TART

6 T butter

3 1/4 c semisweet chocolate chips

3 eggs

1 c granulated sugar

1/2 t vanilla

1 T instant espresso powder

1/2 c all-purpose flour

1/4 t baking powder

1/4 t salt

1 c walnuts, chopped

2 to 3 T heavy cream

Preheat oven to 350° F. Lightly grease and flour 9-inch tart pan with removable sides.

In small heatproof bowl set over saucepan with simmering water, melt butter. Add 2 cups of chocolate chips and remove from heat. Stir until chocolate melts. Set aside to cool completely.

In bowl of stand mixer fitted with paddle attachment, beat eggs, sugar, espresso powder and vanilla on medium-high speed until light and fluffy (about 3 minutes). Stir in cooled chocolate.

In separate medium bowl, combine flour, baking powder, salt, 1 cup of chocolate chips and walnuts. Fold the flour mixture into the batter, until just combined.

Pour batter into prepared tart pan. Bake for 35 to 40 minutes, or until the center is puffed (top may crack slightly). Let brownie tart cool to room temperature before removing from tart pan.

Melt remaining 1/4 cup chocolate chips with the heavy cream in a small saucepan over medium-low heat. Stir until smooth and remove from heat. Drizzle over tart and slice into 8 wedges.

Brownie Points

If you don't have a tart pan, use a standard 9-inch pie pan as a substitute.

ABOUT THE AUTHOR

Harvey Morris lives in Chicago with his four (!) pugs. In 2007, he launched a blog called Baked Chicago in homage to the city that takes good food and innovation very seriously. Strong reader response to the blog's brownie recipes led to this cookbook – a natural for a passionate baker from Chicago, where brownies were first created as a special confection for attendees at the Columbian Exposition of 1893!

Harvey is also passionate about supporting two Chicago organizations that tirelessly help those who are hungry and in need of shelter: the Greater Chicago Food Depository and PAWS Chicago.

*Baked Chicago is proud to donate 100% of the net proceeds from the sale of **Baked Chicago's Simply Decadent Brownies Cookbook** to the Greater Chicago Food Depository and PAWS Chicago.*

For more information, visit these resources:

- ***Baked Chicago** at www.BakedChicago.com*
- ***Greater Chicago Food Depository** at www.ChicagosFoodBank.org*
- ***PAWS Chicago** at www.PAWSChicago.org*

Made in the USA
Las Vegas, NV
15 August 2022

53345199R00043